Nature Upclose

A Slug's Life

Written and Illustrated by John Himmelman

Children's Press®
A Division of Grolier Publishing
New York London Hong Kong Sydney
Danbury, Connecticut

For my friend, Frank Gallo,
who runs wild with the weasels.

Library of Congress Cataloging-in-Publication Data

Himmelman, John
    A slug's life / John Himmelman
        p.   cm. — (Nature upclose)
    Summary: Describes the daily activities and life cycle of a
slug.
        ISBN 0-516-20822-5 (lib. bdg.)   0-516-26356-0 (pbk.)
        1. Slugs (Mollusks)—Juvenile literature.   [1. Slugs
(Mollusks)]   I. Title. II. Series: Himmelman, John.
Nature Upclose
QL430.4.H55   1997
594'.3—dc21
                                                    97-29322
                                                        CIP
                                                         AC

Visit Children's Press on the Internet at:
    http://publishing.grolier.com

Slug
Limax

Slugs are closely related to snails. They both have shells, but a slug's shell is hidden under its skin. Land slugs live in moist places. They spend the day under stones and come out at night to feed. Slugs eat a variety of plants and mushrooms.

There is no such thing as a male slug or a female slug. Every slug is a *hermaphrodite* (her MA fro dyt)—sometimes it acts like a male and sometimes it acts like a female. All slugs can lay eggs.

As slugs move from place to place, they leave behind a slimy trail. The slime is similar to the mucus that runs down the back of your throat when you have a cold. The thick, slippery slime is produced by a gland in the slug's foot. The slime makes it easier for the slug to glide along the ground.

The next time you spot a slug's slime trail, see if you can follow it to the slug's hideout.

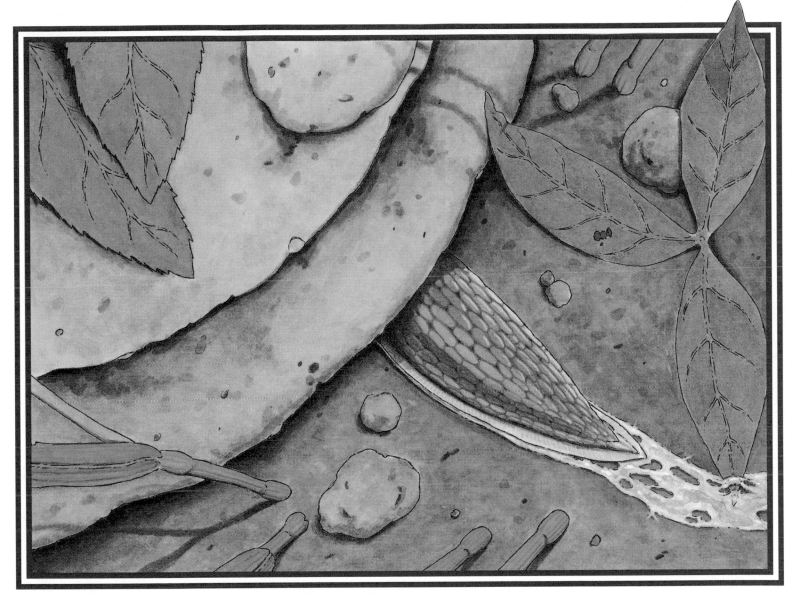

On a moonlit spring night, a slug slips under a damp rock.

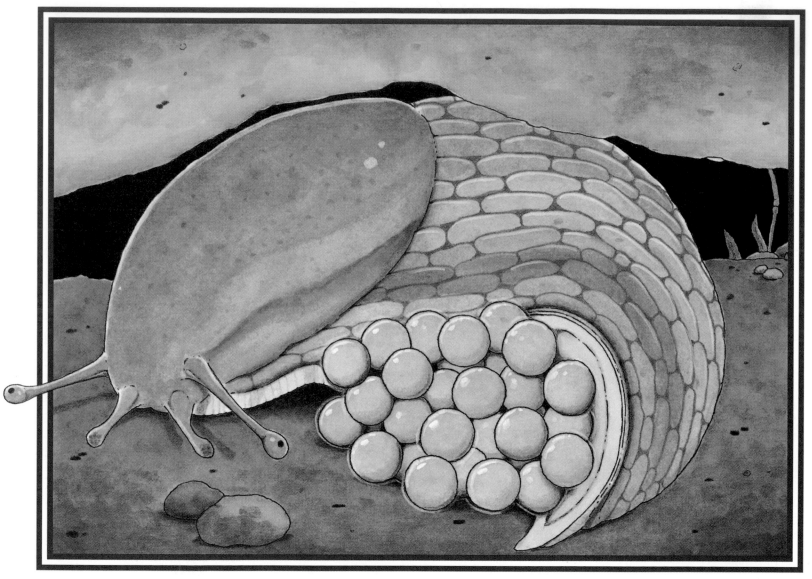

The slug lays a *cluster* of *eggs*.

A young slug begins to grow inside each one.

After a few weeks, the first slug hatches.

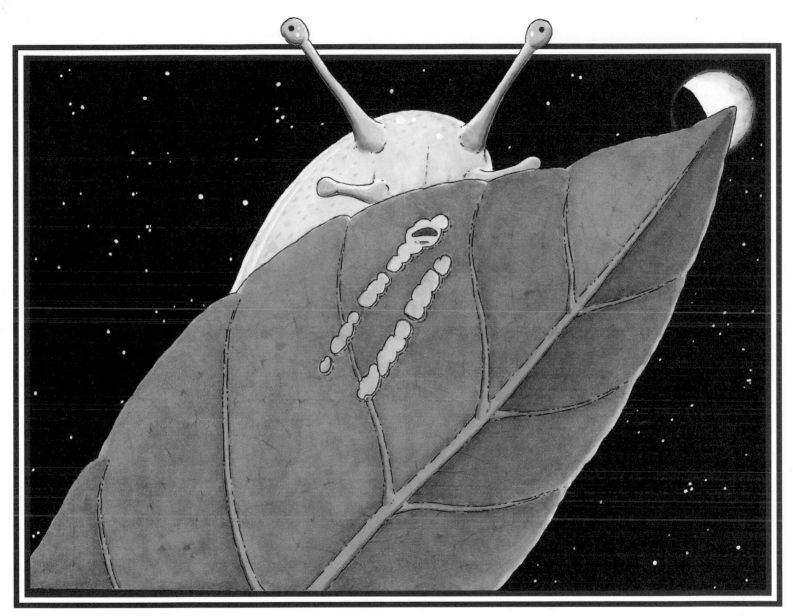

It searches for tender young leaves to eat.

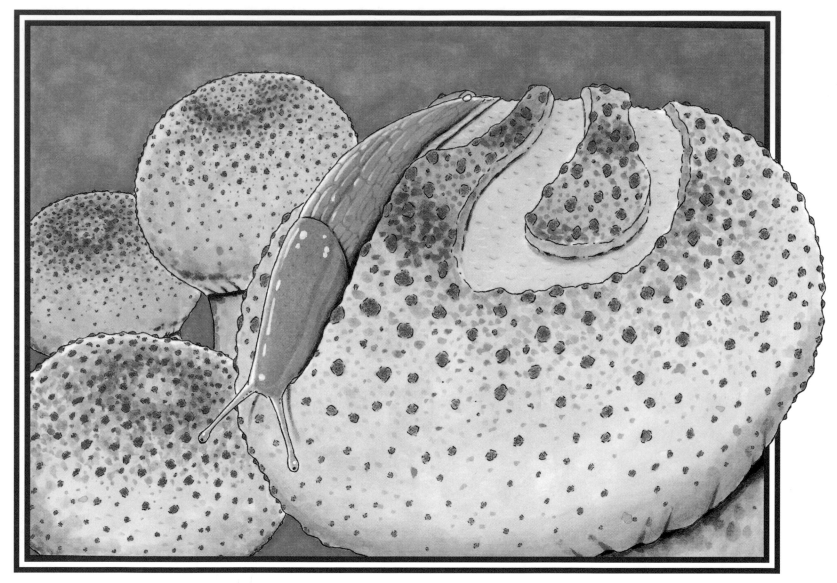

By early summer, the slug has grown darker.
It eats a *puffball mushroom.*

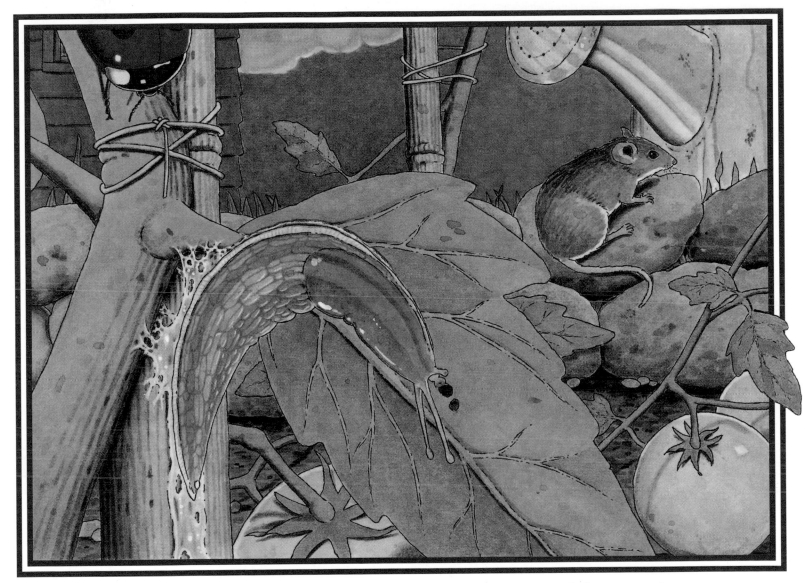

The slug spends its nights feasting in a vegetable garden.

One night, the slug smells something new.

It leaves the garden and begins a dangerous journey.

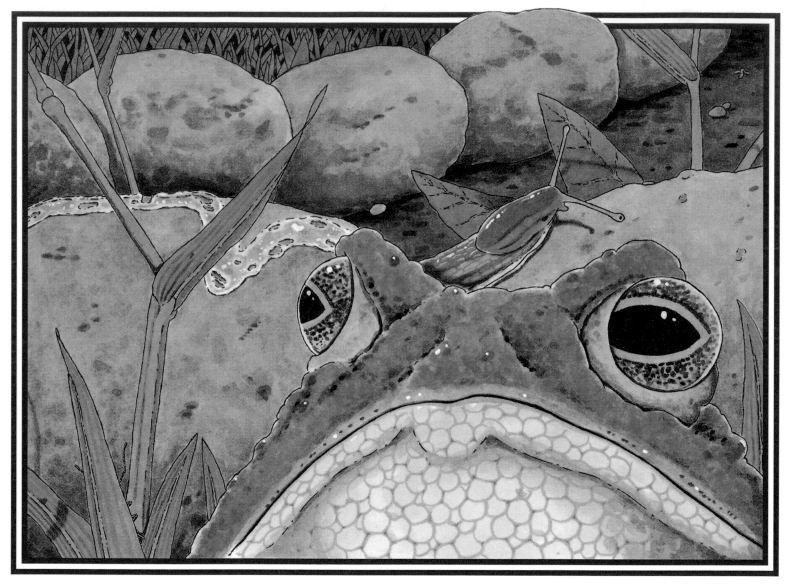

Slugs are an *American toad*'s favorite food!

The slug moves silently and slowly. It sneaks past its enemy.

At last, the slug finds what it is looking for. Cat food makes a tasty meal!

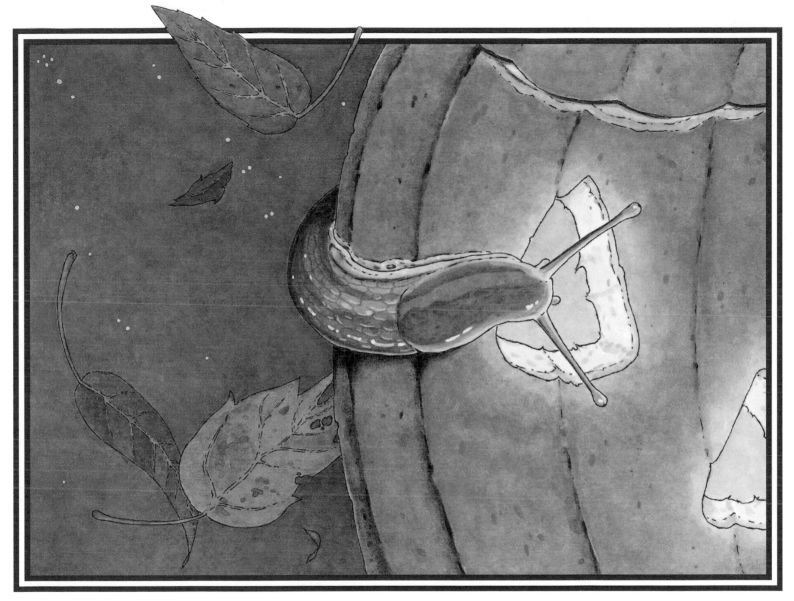

The slug is full grown by late autumn.

The slug does not like cold weather.

It spends the winter underground.

By spring, the slug is very thirsty. It soaks up water from a puddle.

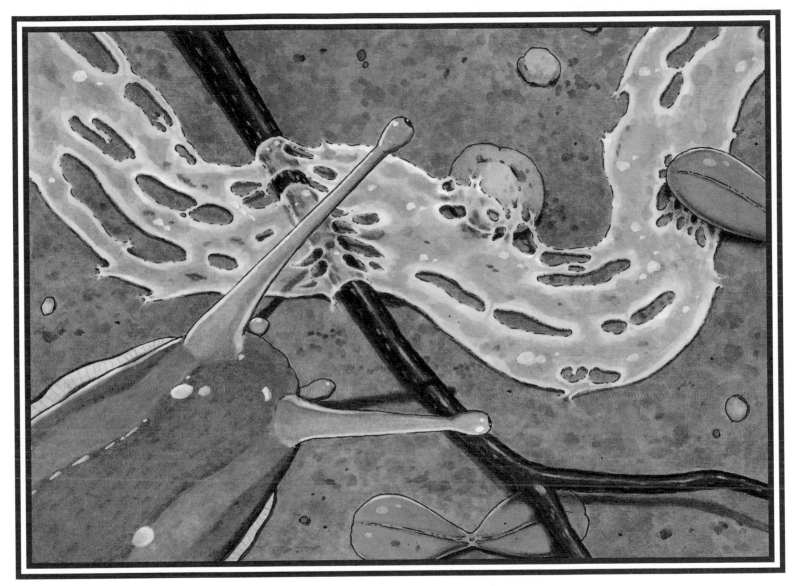

A few nights later, the slug finds a trail of *slime*.

The slug follows the trail . . .

. . . until it meets another slug. The slugs circle, then mate.

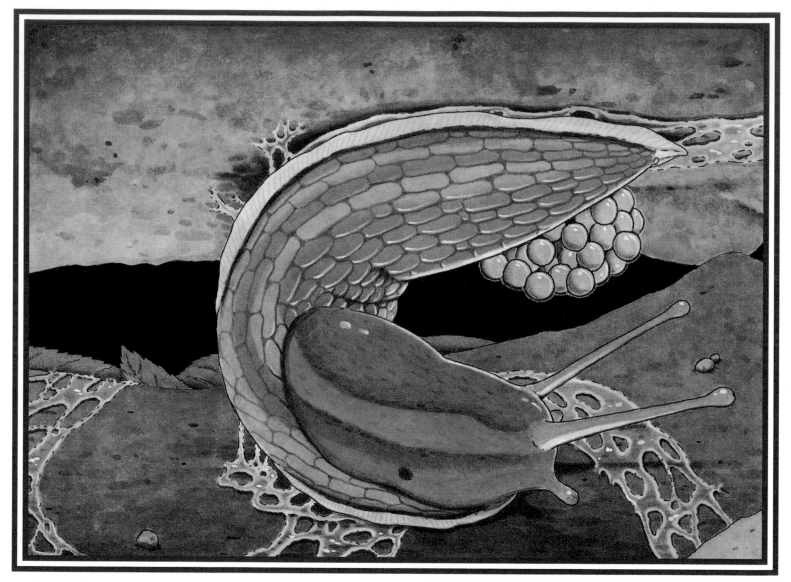

The slug lays its eggs on the bottom of a rock.

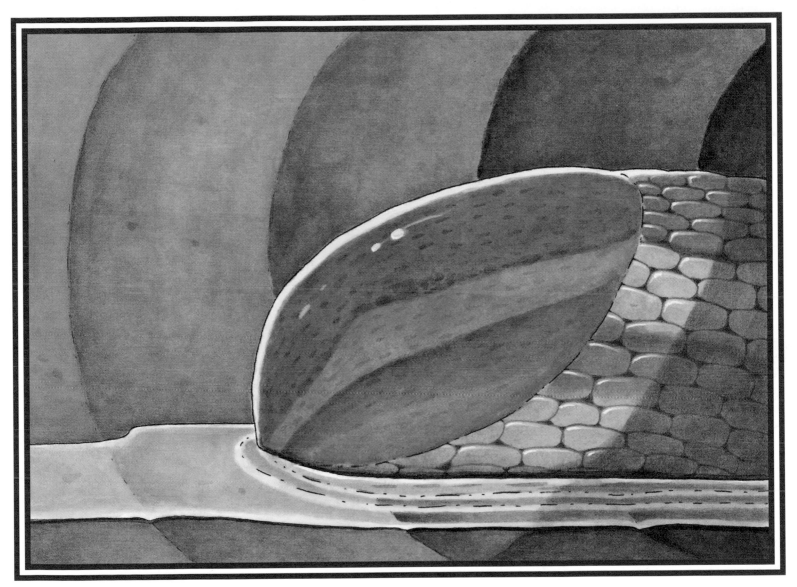

It finds a cool wet place to escape the sun's heat.

The slug's new home is lifted into the air.

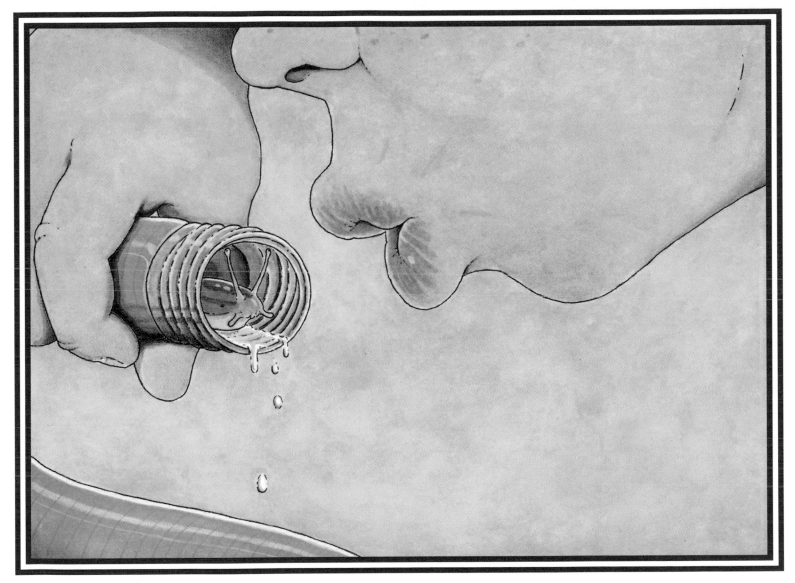

The slug senses danger, but there is no place to hide!

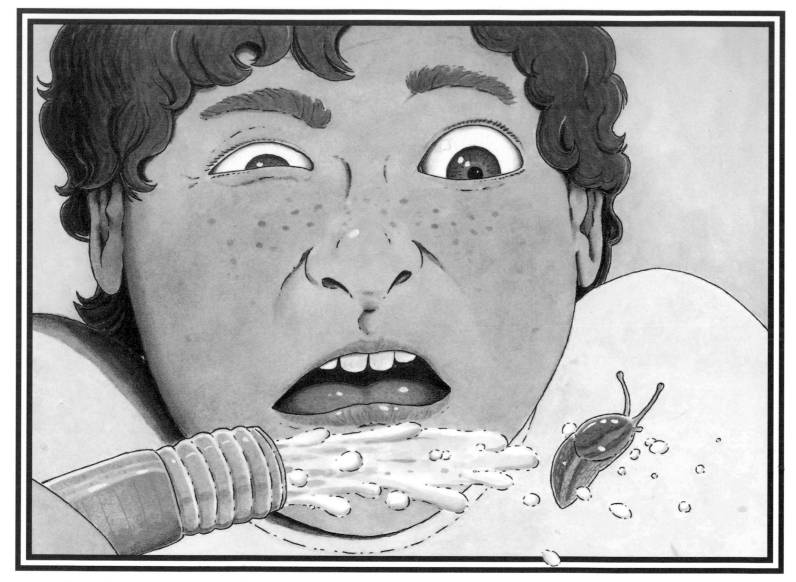

Suddenly, a river of water shoots the slug past a child's lips.

The slug lands in the grass and spots a new slime trail.

The slug follows the trail to a damp dark place. It's perfect for hot summer days.

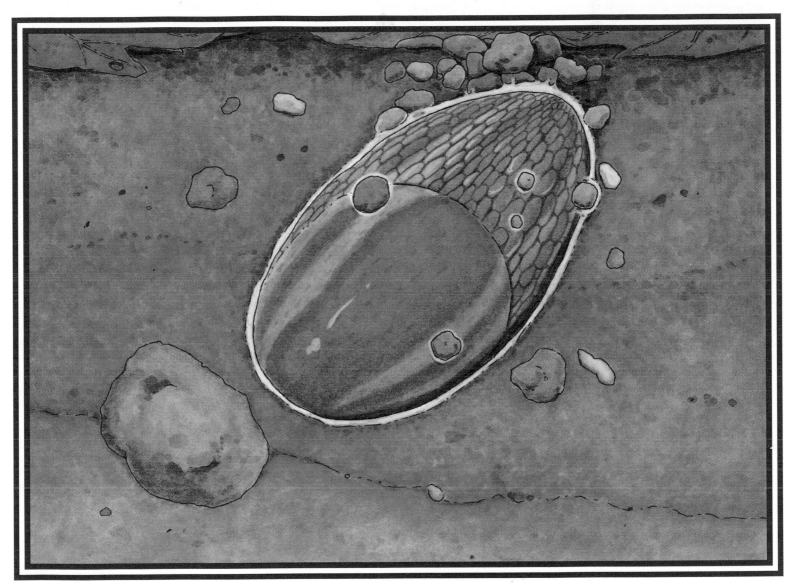

When the cold winter returns, the slug burrows underground.

And when spring arrives, the slug will have new adventures.

Words You Know

American toad—a toad found in most parts of the United States. All toads spend their lives on land.

cluster—a group of similar things found in one place.

egg—the hard protective layer that surrounds a developing creature. Young birds, frogs, insects, and slugs all hatch from eggs.

hermaphrodite—a creature that can act like either a male or a female.

slime—a thick, wet, slippery substance produced by a gland in a slug's foot.

puffball mushroom—the part of a fungus that drops spores. The spore of a mushroom is like the seed of a plant. A spore can grow into a new fungus.

About the Author

John Himmelman has written or illustrated more than forty books for children, including *Ibis: A True Whale Story*, *Wanted: Perfect Parents*, and *J.J. Versus the Babysitter*. His books have received honors such as Pick of the List, Book of the Month, JLG Selection, and the ABC Award. He is also a naturalist who enjoys turning over dead logs, crawling through grass, kneeling over puddles, and gazing at the sky. His greatest joy is sharing these experiences with others. John lives in Killingworth, Connecticut, with his wife Betsy who is an art teacher. They have two children, Jeff and Liz.